EAT TO LIVE

Susan Steinlauf

Copyright June 8, 2011

Dedication

For all the great cooks and eaters in my family who taught me to
appreciate the importance of presenting healthy, nutritious meals
that both taste good and look beautiful when served.

Table of Contents

Table of Contents

Introduction

Imagine sitting in your doctor's office and hearing the news that you have a serious disease characterized by fatty deposits, inflammation and scar tissue covering 75% of your liver. Your doctor tells you that to avoid a more serious condition that would lead to a transplant solution, you had to lose enough weight to burn out all the fat surrounding your belly to reduce the inflammation and eventually allow your scar tissue to heal. You are referred to other specialists who test for insulin resistance, cholesterol levels, weight management and fitness level.

You discover you have a condition called Metabolic Syndrome; a typically hereditary illness characterized by excessive belly fat with a waistline exceeding 35" for women, and 40" for men, with 2-3 additional factors including heart disease, high blood pressure, high cholesterol and Diabetes.

This scenario was true for me, and I had a serious liver illness that was complicated by Metabolic Syndrome thanks to high cholesterol, history of maternal family heart disease and borderline type-2 Diabetes. I consulted with a variety of specialists, but was determined not to try any program that I knew from experience would set me up to fail; that is, regain the weight and inches once the weight loss phase ended.

Dr. Mayer and Mrs. Karen Eisenstein are family; Karen is my husband's first cousin. I nearly dropped my jaw when I saw them in our frozen yogurt shop in mid-February, 2011 as Mayer had lost over 100 lbs., and Karen had lost 70 lbs.! They both looked and said they felt absolutely fantastic! Mayer told us about his low-Glycemic Index diet plan currently in use in his medical practice, called Homefirst. His program features 30 day phases of a 500 calorie (Very Low Calorie Diet) based on Dr. Simeon's book Pounds and Inches, including his proprietary formula for sub-lingual doses of Human Chorionic Gonadotropin (HCG) which is a hormone naturally produced by pregnant women, and a variety of proprietary nutritional supplements. HCG phases are followed by periods of maintenance lasting from 30 days to several months. Mayer explained that the maintenance phases allow the metabolic system to acclimate to the physical weight loss, while giving the person's mind a chance to accept the new reality before starting another HCG phase. This was the program I'd been looking for! The big problem was trying to figure out how to eat the foods allowed on the diet in the quantities prescribed without feeling deprived or completely bored with what seemed like a very narrow list of items.

My husband decided to support me by following the program with me, and we realized that our daughter would benefit from the dietary changes too.

Prepared foods from grocery or specialty stores were suddenly and permanently off the table, which was a considerable hardship given our very busy lifestyle. It became apparent that I'd need to prepare home-cooked meals for my family much more regularly and needed to find ways to use the recommended foods on the Homefirst VLCD in new combinations.

I searched the Internet and cookbooks on my shelves for recipes using fruits, vegetables, and lean sources of protein and was surprised to find that many were loaded with ingredients I could no longer enjoy on the HCG phase, and should also avoid during maintenance. I also missed many of my favorite dishes made with most legumes, pasta, rice or potatoes. So, I got creative and started trying my favorite recipes with substitutions from the list of approved foods and those with the lowest numbers on the Glycemic Index for use while on maintenance.

The result of my efforts is this compilation of a variety of recipes that I've made at home for my family and friends who agree they're delicious. Some are appropriate for both the HCG and maintenance phases, others for short and long-term weight maintenance.

Feel free to experiment and modify or adapt them to your tastes until they become your family favorites! Where the recipe calls for you to "season to taste", that means to add salt or any seasoning mix you like and may use depending on your health. Enjoy!

Recipes for the HCG Phase

Condiments and Sauces

DIPPING SAUCE FOR STEAMED ASPARAGUS
HCG Phase

1 Lemon, juiced
1 Tsp. Dijon Mustard
2-3 Tsp. Capers
2 Tsp. White Wine Vinegar
1/8 Tsp. dried Tarragon or any dried herbs

Mix all ingredients in a small bowl or ramekin.
Serve with steamed Artichokes or as a topping for steamed or grilled asparagus.

Recipe makes enough dip for 1 lb. asparagus.

One night we were invited to have dinner in the home of some friends we knew quite well. Our hostess wanted to make a fresh tomato salad but was busy preparing something else. I offered to whip up a batch of Bruschetta; essentially a tomato, basil, garlic and olive oil mixture typically served spooned over thickly sliced, toasted Italian bread. Then I mixed up some garlic butter spread and coated the top of some slices of the bread she planned to serve with the salad, and toasted it. Her family flipped when they tasted it, so at her request, I wrote everything down so she could prepare it. And she did make it, too, the next time we got together!

This recipe, without the garlic buttered bread, works very well as a topping for chicken or pork chops, steak or fish. I even like it tossed in salad instead of using dressing!

ITALIAN STYLE BRUSHCETTA
HCG Phase

4-6 Roma Tomatoes, finely diced
2 Tbl. Basil, fresh chopped
1-2 Cloves Garlic, fresh crushed or finely minced more or less to taste
1-2 Tsp. Red Onion, finely minced if desired
2 Tsp. Balsamic Vinegar
1/8 Tsp. Red Chili Flakes if desired
1-2 Tsp. Capers if desired
Season to taste

Chop or mince each of the first 4 ingredients and place in a bowl.
Add vinegar, chili flakes and capers if desired to taste.
Mix well.
Taste mixture to adjust amount of seasonings, and to test spiciness of the garlic and chili flakes.

Refrigerate for at least 30 minutes before serving.

Recipe makes 8 servings.

Serving Suggestions:
Spoon onto Melba Toast, 2 pieces equals 1 serving.
Use as a condiment on steak, broiled chicken or fish.

In Memphis, the Dry Rub is the most important ingredient aside from the meat. This means that this barbecue rub has to provide the flavor to make Memphis Style Barbecue.

This rub starts with a generous portion of paprika and then builds a slightly spicy but definitely savory profile to help you make the most of your barbecue. This Memphis Rub is great on steaks, chops, chicken (and ribs) especially when smoked.

MEMPHIS DRY RUB BARBECUE SPICE MIX
HCG Phase and Maintenance

1/2 Cup Paprika
1/4 Cup Garlic powder
1/4 Cup mild Chili Powder (use medium or hot to kick up the heat)
3 Tbl. Salt
3 Tbl. Black Pepper
2 Tbl. Onion Powder
2 Tbl. Celery Seeds
1 Tbl. Truvia Sweetener
1 Tbl. Dried Oregano
1 Tbl. Dried Thyme
1 Tbl. Cumin
2 Tsp. Dry Mustard
2 Tsp. Ground Coriander
2 Tsp. Ground Allspice

Mix all ingredients together and store in an airtight container or use a large empty jar or bottle!

Recipe makes 13 oz. of spice mix.

We love chopped Italian style tomato relish, but eat Mexican salsa with everything. This recipe can be tailored to your taste, and be spicy or mild or in between! We sometimes roast the vegetables before chopping them, and sometimes chop them raw but we always enjoy the results. I hope you will, too!

MEXICAN SALSA
HCG Phase and Maintenance

4 Roma Tomatoes, finely diced
2 Tbl. Onion, finely minced
½ Jalapeno Pepper, finely minced more or less to taste
2 Tbl. Cilantro leaves, chopped
Season to taste
1 Lime, juiced

Chop or mince each of the first 4 ingredients and place in a bowl.
Add seasonings and lime juice.
Mix well.
Taste salsa to adjust amount of salt or lime, and to test spiciness of the Jalapeno pepper; milder or hotter peppers may also be used.
If the pepper makes the salsa too spicy, add more tomato, onion and cilantro.

Use as a condiment on Carne Asada or other Mexican style dishes or on steak, broiled chicken or fish.

Recipe makes 8 servings.

Additional ingredients:
Add 1 diced ripe avocado during the Maintenance Phase only.
Use 1 Tbl. vinegar in place of lime for a different taste.

Alternate preparation method for Fire-roasted Salsa:
Roast tomatoes chili pepper and onion on a barbecue or in a heavy non-stick skillet on the stove until the skins turn dark. Peel the tomatoes and chili.
Place all ingredients in a food processor and pulse-process gently.

Entrees for Lunch or Dinner

Ceviche is a simple, elegant and very fresh way to prepare fish. It can be spicy or tart, or a little of both! It is a great dish to serve when the weather is warm because it must be chilled thoroughly from the time it is prepared until it is ready to eat. Ceviche makes a great appetizer, lunch or dinner entrée, and is fun to make with either fish or shrimp, or both!

CEVICHE
HCG Phase

1-1/2 lbs. fresh fish; Halibut, Snapper or Sea Bass
10 Roma tomatoes, diced
1 whole onion, finely diced
1 bunch cilantro leaves, finely chopped
4-6 Limes, juiced
½ - 1 whole Jalapeno pepper, finely diced
Season to taste

Dice fish into bite-sized chunks and place in a non-metallic bowl.
Cut the tomatoes, onion, Jalapeno and cilantro and add to the bowl.
Juice the limes and add to the mixture, then add salt to taste.
Refrigerate covered for 8 hours or until the fish is completely
marinated.

Serve chilled.

Recipe makes 6 servings.

Variation:
Substitute shrimp for the fish. Cook shrimp by poaching them first
in water using a pan with a lid. Use enough water to cover the
surface of the pan by ½ inch on high heat, and cook the shrimp until
the shells or outer skin turns pink.

I was blessed to know both my grandmothers very well, and learned a great deal about life, as well as how to cook many of our family's favorite foods. Both of them were masters in the art of making traditional chicken soup, and I learned all their secrets!

My cousin, a professional chef, taught me another lesson; to cook the broth uncovered to allow it to reduce to make it taste stronger before adding more water and the vegetables. The traditional version my grandmothers made differs from this recipe because I omit carrots and add zucchini and tomatoes to the parsley, onion and celery to make a Chicken Vegetable soup on the HCG Phase.

Chicken soup is more than a meal; for me it is also a link from all the generations of women in my family that came before me to the generations that will follow. It is everything it's cracked up to be, from a healing elixir for the body to a salve for the soul. Chicken soup is made with love above all else, and this simple recipe is a gift from me to you!

CHICKEN VEGETABLE SOUP
HCG Phase

1 Whole Chicken, Kosher preferred, washed thoroughly
3 Stalks Celery, trimmed
1 Yellow Onion, peeled and quartered
2 Whole Zucchini, cut into thick chunks
1 Bunch Parsley, kept together with a rubber band or string
2 Roma Tomatoes
1 lb. Mushrooms, any variety, trimmed
Season to taste

Place washed chicken in an 8 qt. pot and fill with water until the chicken is almost covered.
Bring to a boil for 20-30 minutes.
Skim the scum that forms at the top of the pot.
Reduce the heat to medium and continue boiling uncovered for another 15 minutes. Add whole stalks celery, zucchini chunks, one quartered yellow onion, mushrooms and a bunch of parsley.
Cover and reduce heat to low, simmering for 40 minutes.
Remove chicken, add seasonings and continue to simmer uncovered on medium heat for another 15 minutes.
When the chicken is cool, remove the bones and skin.
Return the chicken to the soup and add the diced tomatoes.
Cook for another 5 minutes uncovered.
Skim all the fat before serving.

Note: If you don't need to serve this soup immediately, refrigerate it until the fat hardens, then remove it!

EGG FOO YOUNG
HCG Phase

3 Eggs; one yolk and all egg whites
½ Cup Bean Sprouts
3 Stalks Asparagus
1 or 2 Baby Bok Choy
¼ Onion or 2 Scallions
2-3 Mushrooms
3-4 Snap Peas or Chinese Pea Pods

Rough chop all vegetables, add others or subtract the ones you don't like or have on hand!
Steam or microwave all the vegetables except bean sprouts until soft.
Scramble eggs, stir in the vegetables.
Cook like a pancake in a non-stick skillet until the eggs are firm enough to flip, cook on the other side until done.

Recipe makes 1 serving.

The idea of cooking stewed tomatoes with eggs nearly made me sick when I was a college student, but my roommate grew up loving this traditional Sephardic recipe at breakfast. She encouraged me to taste it, and I must admit that it was absolutely delicious. I still remember that morning, 30 years later!

So try it, you'll like it!

EGGS WITH STEWED TOMATOES
HCG Phase

1 14-16 oz. Can Tomatoes, stewed or diced
3 Eggs; 2 whites only, 1 with yolk
1 Clove Garlic, crushed
Season to taste
Dried Oregano or other dried herbs to taste

Place canned tomatoes, crushed garlic, salt, pepper and herbs into a
2-3 quart pot and heat until it boils.
Crack open, separate and remove yolks from 2 eggs while allowing
whites to fall into a bowl.
Open all 3 eggs and drop into the bubbling tomatoes.
Cover and reduce heat to low and cook until the egg yolks have cooked
to your liking.
Remove 2 of the cooked yolks and discard.
Spoon tomatoes and eggs into a bowl to serve.

Recipe makes 1 serving.

Summertime in Southern California means cooking dinner on the grill at our house! We put everything on our barbecue, from steaks, chops, fish and chicken to vegetables, even romaine lettuce for a fantastic salad.

Asparagus is my favorite vegetable, with green beans coming in a close second place. Both can be simply seasoned and sprayed with olive oil before cooking on the grill. Go ahead; try grilling your favorite vegetable!

GRILLED ASPARAGUS
HCG Phase

1 lb. Asparagus, fresh
Season to taste

Wash asparagus and trim off the tough ends.
Soak the asparagus for a few minutes in water.
Spread the spears across a platter to form one layer.
Sprinkle with seasonings to taste.
Grill on a low heat turning as they cook.
Remove from the grill when lightly browned, place spears onto the platter.

Alternate Vegetable selections, omit the soaking step:
Slice zucchini into $\frac{3}{4}$" –1" thick pieces
Slice onions into $\frac{1}{2}$" thick rings
Slice any color bell peppers into strips
Snip root end off scallions

GRILLED ASPARAGUS (Indoor Method)
HCG Phase

1 lb. Asparagus, fresh

Wash asparagus and trim off the tough ends.
Spread the spears across a platter to form one layer.
Moisten with a spray of water; any pump style spritzer will work.
Flip the asparagus and spray the other side.
Cook in a non-stick grill or sauté pan on a medium heat turning as they cook.
Remove from the grill when lightly browned, place spears onto the platter.
Season cooked vegetables with lemon, spices and herbs if desired.

Alternate Vegetable selections:
Slice zucchini into $\frac{3}{4}$" –1" thick pieces and prepare as above.
Slice onions into $\frac{1}{2}$" thick rings and prepare as above.
Slice any color bell peppers into strips and prepare as above.
Snip root end off scallions and prepare as above.

I rarely order chicken dishes in restaurants because I cook chicken at home so often. This recipe for grilled lemon-mustard chicken is good enough to be on anybody's menu!

Here's another twist on the following recipe for Lemon Dijon Chicken: Begin with 2 boneless, skinless chicken breasts. Pound the chicken nearly flat with a tenderizer tool. Marinate for a couple of hours in a sauce containing 1 whole clove of minced garlic, 4 Tbl. of Extra-virgin Olive Oil, 1 Tsp. of Dijon mustard, a tablespoon of chopped fresh rosemary, from $\frac{1}{2}$ to 1 whole Tsp. of crushed red chili flakes and a splash of dry white wine and/or chicken broth, salt to taste. Cook the marinated chicken on a hot grill until done on both sides, but take care not to overcook!

GRILLED LEMON DIJON CHICKEN
HCG Phase and Maintenance

4 Chicken Breasts, skinless, boneless
$\frac{1}{4}$ Cup Lemon juice
$\frac{1}{2}$ Tbl. Lemon zest, finely chopped
1/8 Cup Dijon (any variety) Mustard
1/8 cup Fresh herbs-any combination of Rosemary, Thyme, Basil,
Oregano, Parsley or Italian Parsley, finely chopped
1/8 Tsp. Crushed Red Pepper

Combine marinade ingredients in a small bowl, mix well.
Arrange chicken pieces in a large shallow non-aluminum dish and pour marinade over them.
Marinate 2-4 hours in the refrigerator.
Heat barbecue for medium heat grilling.
Place the chicken breasts onto the grill and discard the marinade.
Cook 7-10 minutes on each side.
Serve hot or refrigerate after cooling and slice the chicken to top a chilled green salad.

Recipe makes 8 servings during the HCG Phase; 4 servings during the Maintenance Phase.

Alternatives:
Use 1 lb. chicken tenders in place of boneless breasts, add $\frac{1}{2}$ Cup of Chicken Broth to the marinade before cooking with chopped vegetables in a non-stick pan with a lid.

Prepare boneless chicken per the recipe; add 8 oz. sliced mushrooms of any variety into the marinade. Place the chicken in a covered roasting pan or Dutch/French oven and sprinkle the tops with Paprika before adding the marinade to the pan.
Bake at 375 degrees until fully cooked.

LEMON TARRAGON CHICKEN CASSOULET
HCG PHASE

4 skinless chicken breasts with ribs attached.
4-6 cloves garlic, whole
3 stalks fresh Tarragon, chopped or 3 Tbl. Dried Tarragon
1 onion, chopped
2 Cups Asparagus, whole or sliced
2 Cups mushrooms, whole
2 Cups Spinach leaves
2 Roma Tomatoes, sliced in quarters
3 lemons, sliced in half
½ Cup good water
1 Cup non-fat, low sodium Chicken Broth
Salt and Pepper to taste

Clean chicken inside and out and season well.
Place chicken in a Dutch or French oven or heavy pot with lid.
Slice lemons in half and stuff the cavity of the chicken with as many as will fit inside.
Bake at 350 degrees for 20 minutes uncovered.
Add the remaining lemons, wine, broth Tarragon, garlic, and onions to the pot. Bake covered for 20 minutes.
Add mushrooms; continue cooking for another 10 minutes.
Add asparagus, spinach and tomatoes, cook for another 10 minutes.
Remove the chicken breasts from the pot and cut in half, removing bones; place the chicken in a large serving bowl.
Remove all the vegetables from the pot with a slotted spoon and surround the chicken with them.
Drain all the pan juices into a gravy-fat separator or into a 4-cup measuring cup.
Remove any fat and debris as possible, and pour the remaining juices over the chicken and vegetables.

Recipe makes 8 servings.

PORK TENDERLOIN ITALIAN STYLE
HCG Phase and Maintenance

Whole Pork Tenderloin, trimmed and skinless
Garlic Powder
Basil, dried
Oregano, dried
Onion, thinly sliced if using an oven

Season the pork.
Cook on a grill at medium heat without the onions, or roast in the oven using a covered roasting pan (use foil if your pan doesn't have a lid).
To cook in the oven, layer the bottom of a roasting pan with thinly sliced onions and add 2 Tbl. of water, place the meat on top of the onions, and cook covered in the oven, preheated to 350 degrees.
Cook the Tenderloin until medium-well done using a meat thermometer.
Let the meat rest for 10 minutes before slicing.
Tenderloin should be white and very moist; if it's pink in the middle when test-sliced; then return it to the oven until done and the juices run clear.
Once doneness is confirmed, remove from the grill or roasting pan and slice into strips.
Fan the meat on the plate and top with fresh Bruschetta (see the recipe on page 55; omit Olive Oil if you're on the HCG Phase).

SASHIMI FISH TACOS
HCG Phase

4 oz. Sashimi grade fresh fish; Ahi Tuna or Yellowtail
3 large Butter Lettuce leaves, Red or Green Leaf or Romaine
3 Mushrooms, any variety
2 Scallions
½ Cup Ponzu Sauce, bottled or freshly made
Crushed Red Chili Pepper flakes to taste
3 Asparagus spears, steamed and trimmed

Position lettuce leaves on a plate.
Pour bottled Ponzu sauce (or make your own with ¼ cup of gluten free or low sodium soy sauce mixed with ¼ cup rice wine vinegar and 1 Tbl. lemon juice) into a bowl and add crushed Red Chili Pepper flakes if desired.
Gently steam the trimmed asparagus until slightly crisp and tender.
Slice the fresh fish into thin strips or small chunks.
Trim and slice the mushrooms and scallions.
Toss the fish, mushrooms and diced scallions into the Ponzu sauce.
Position the mixture onto the lettuce leaves and top with the asparagus.
Fold the lettuce to wrap the toppings into a taco and enjoy!

Recipe makes 1 serving.

I just love the months that end with the letter "r". That means its shellfish season! The grocer in our neighborhood displays fresh lobster, crab, shrimp, clams and mussels at this time of year at reasonable prices so I like to treat my family to this recipe for seafood stew. I hope you like it too!

SEAFOOD STEW
HCG Phase

4 C Seafood Stock
½ lb. Crab (King, Dungeness or Snow, in shell)
½ lb. Shrimp, peeled and deveined
1 Filet of fresh fish, 8 oz., diced
1 Onion, diced
2-4 Cloves Garlic, fresh, chopped to taste
2 Stalks Celery, diced
Season to taste

Heat 1 cup stock in stock pot and add garlic, onion and celery.
Cook until soft.
Add remaining stock and seasonings, bring to a boil.
Reduce heat to low, and add crab for about 5 minutes.
Add mussels and clams, cover and cook for another 3 minutes.
Add shrimp and continue cooking until fish is cooked and clams and mussels open, about 2-3 more minutes.
=Remove crab and slice open the legs vertically in half to make it easy to remove the meat, return crab to the pot.
This dish can be served from the pot, or can be transferred to a large deep bowl.

Recipe makes about 5 four-ounce portions depending on the yield of the meat from the crab.

SHRIMP IN LETTUCE TACOS
HCG Phase and Maintenance

4 oz. Shrimp (or Crabmeat or Lobster, or any cooked white fish)
3 Butter Lettuce leafs, Red or Green Leaf or Romaine
$\frac{1}{2}$ Cup Water and $\frac{1}{2}$ Cup Vinegar, any White Wine Type
2-3 Tbl. Old Bay seasoning
3-4 Tbl. Mexican Salsa
Cabbage, finely shredded
Lime Slices

Steam the shrimp (or other seafood with the shell) in the boiling water and vinegar with seasoning until the shell turns pink in a covered pan.
Drain and cool, then peel the shrimp.
Arrange the shrimp on the lettuce leafs; add salsa and cabbage, then top with a squeeze of lime.
Fold the lettuce leaves into a taco, and enjoy!

Variation:
Mix diced chicken or chicken tenders with Walden Farms Barbecue sauce and topping it with sliced dill pickles.
Sprinkle 2 chicken tenders with any seasoning, cook in the microwave for 2 minutes or poach in a covered pan with water or broth.

SHRIMP SALAD
HCG Phase

4 oz. Shrimp
1 Cup Salad Greens
¼ Radicchio
1 Belgian Endive
1 Roma Tomato (or other tomato types)
1 Scallion, finely sliced
2 Mushrooms, fresh, sliced
1 Stalk Celery, peeled and sliced
½ Grapefruit (do not use grapefruit if you take a Statin medication to reduce high cholesterol) or a whole Orange, peeled, sectioned and sliced in half; or use 1 Cup cut Strawberries

Steam the shrimp with the method used to make Shrimp Tacos. Toss them into a bowl on top of mixed salad greens with radicchio and endive, diced Roma tomatoes, diced scallion, fresh mushrooms, and celery sliced as thinly as possible and cut fruit sections.
Dress the salad with a mixture of lemon juice and white wine or Sherry vinegar, and a variety of dried herbs and toss well.

Optional Dressing:
Fat/sugar free Italian dressing by Walden Farms, or Walden Farms Thousand Island dressing if you don't use fruit.

STUFFED MUSHROOMS
HCG Phase

6 Medium Portobello Mushrooms suitable for stuffing
6 oz. Chicken Breast or Turkey Breast, chopped or ground
1 Can Tomatoes, whole and skinless
1/2 Onion, thinly sliced
2-3 Cloves Garlic, fresh, crushed to taste
2 Stalks Celery, finely diced
6 Asparagus spears, cut up into $\frac{1}{2}$" slices
$\frac{1}{2}$ Zucchini, shredded or processed
1 Cup Spinach, steamed in the microwave for 1 minute
1 Handful of Basil, fresh, finely chopped or 1 Tbl. dried
Season to taste

Pull out the stems of the mushrooms, and place into a glass or other microwaveable cooking dish.
Microwave cook the mushrooms covered with paper towels or a paper plate for 4-5 minutes until done.
Using a 5 qt. pot, crush up the tomatoes by hand; add the juice in the can.
Drain and add the juice from the mushrooms, the spinach, garlic, zucchini, asparagus, basil and the seasonings.
Bring to a rapid simmer, and lower the heat to a gentile simmer until all the vegetables are soft.
Return the mushrooms to the cooking dish.
Stuff the mushrooms with one ounce of cooked poultry, and top all with spoonfuls of the vegetables and sauce.
Bake at 350 degrees or microwave them until totally hot and bubbly.

Recipe makes 3 mushrooms per person.

Fruit Dessert

What's for dessert? That is the biggest question I hear at the dinner table! I like to eat fresh strawberries if I get a sweet tooth after dinner, and haven't already had 2 servings of fruit during the day. Strawberries aren't always in season though, so it comes in handy to have another choice.

 I still have a vivid memory of the time my grandma, who was on Weight-Watchers, made a baked apple using diet black cherry soda.

That was it! Baked apples for dessert! Now I just core an apple, usually a Granny Smith though any type will work, and place it in a glass bowl, then add some non-sugar sweetener to cinnamon and nutmeg and spoon it into the cavity. I cover it with a paper plate and microwave it until the apple is completely soft. Sometimes I bake 4 apples at a time in the oven to have enough of them for my family.

Yum!

BAKED APPLES
HCG Phase and Maintenance

4 Medium Granny Smith Apples
4 Tbl. Ground Cinnamon
1-2 Packets of Truvia, if desired
2 Tsp. Ground Nutmeg
1/4 Tsp. Water for each apple

Preheat oven to 350 degrees.
Remove the core from the apples and place in a baking dish.
Mix cinnamon, nutmeg and sweetener if desired together in a small bowl. Amount of sweetener depends on type and your taste, approximately $\frac{1}{2}$ -1 packet of sweetener per apple.
Pour water into the cavity of each apple and add $\frac{1}{4}$ of the dry mixture.
Bake at 350 degrees until apples are soft and fully cooked; approximately 15-20 minutes.

Variations:
Use Diet Black Cherry soda in place of the Cinnamon, Nutmeg and sweetener.

Sliced Baked Apples:
Double the amount of the dry mixture, and sprinkle it into the baking dish.
Slice the cored apples and lay the slices in the pan.
Sprinkle remaining dry mixture over the top of the apples, and pour 1 Tbl. water over them.
Bake covered at 350 degrees for 15-20 minutes or until fully cooked, or microwave cook them until soft, at least 3 minutes.

FRESH FRUIT COMPOTE
HCG Phase

½ Grapefruit
1 Navel Orange
1 Medium Apple
1 Cup Strawberries

Peel and section the grapefruit and orange; slice each section in half.
Core and slice the apple; cut each piece to bite sized.
Remove stems and slice the strawberries.
Mix all together in a bowl, and chill before serving.

Recipe makes 4 servings.

Variation for Maintenance Phase:
Add ½ cup blueberries, raspberries or blackberries, and peeled sliced kiwi.

Recipes for the Maintenance Phase

Breakfast

I couldn't imagine what I would do with the large container of plain non-fat yogurt sitting on the top shelf of my refrigerator that first day after going on the Maintenance phase of the diet. Given what seemed like a short list of allowed foods, I had seen it on the list and bought it. Oh, I knew it would be good mixed with dill and finely diced cucumbers as I'd seen it served in Greek and Indian restaurants, but darn, I can't digest cucumber. I remembered liking it as a condiment with lentils and rice when I tried adhering to a vegetarian diet in the late 1980's but rice wasn't on the diet plan.

Suddenly it hit me: mix in some sugar free jam and Truvia sugar-substitute and maybe it will be edible! Guess what? It is better than that, it's great! My husband and I love this recipe and enjoy mixing fresh fruit into the yogurt as well. The flavor possibilities are not quite infinite, but have some fun with this one!

ALMOST HOMEMADE FRUIT YOGURT
Maintenance Phase

½ Cup Plain Yogurt, lowfat
2-3 Tbl. Sugar-Free Fruit Jam, any variety
1/8 -1/4 Cup Fruit or Berries, Sliced if practical
4-5 Drops Liquid Stevia or 2 Tsp. Truvia to taste

Mix all ingredients together and enjoy!

Recipe makes 1 serving.

EGG FOO YOUNG
Maintenance Phase

3 Eggs; one yolk and all egg whites
2-3 oz. Cooked Shrimp, Chicken, Lean Pork or Beef, diced or chopped
½ Cup Bean Sprouts
3 Stalks Asparagus
1 or 2 Baby Bok Choy
¼ Onion or 2 Scallions
2-3 Mushrooms
3-4 Snap Peas or Chinese Pea Pods
2 Tsp. Sesame Oil (Optional)

Rough chop all vegetables.
Steam or microwave all the vegetables except bean sprouts until soft.
Cook or reheat leftover meat or shrimp.
Scramble eggs, stir in the vegetables and meat or shrimp.
Cook like a pancake in a non-stick skillet with optional Sesame Oil until the eggs are firm enough to flip, cook on the other side until done.

Recipe makes 1 serving.

Condiments and Sauces

BASIC BARBECUE SAUCE
Maintenance Phase

2 Tbl. Canola Oil
1 Medium Onion, finely chopped
3 Cloves Garlic, minced
1-1/2 Cups Tomato Sauce
½ Cup Cider Vinegar
¼ Cup Worcestershire Sauce
1/3 Cup Truvia sweetener
1 Tbl. Chili Powder
½ Tsp. Red Cayenne Pepper; more to taste for spicier sauce

Heat the oil in a saucepan over moderate heat and add onion and garlic.
Stir while cooking, about 5 minutes.
Add the tomato sauce, vinegar, Worcestershire sauce, Truvia, chili powder
and cayenne pepper.
Reduce the heat and simmer, partially covered, until the sauce has thickened slightly, about 20 minutes.
Set aside ¾ to 1 cup of sauce to pass at the table.
Brush the remaining sauce on chicken, fish or meat while grilling during the last 10-15 minutes of cooking time.

Recipe makes about 2-1/2 Cups.

The artichoke is a very majestic plant that yields one of our favorite and most exotic vegetables. It's important to trim the sharp ends off each leaf and cut off as much of the stem as you can before steaming or grilling them. The leaves become tender when fully cooked and I love the feeling of the pulp sliding off the leaves between my teeth. Traditionally served with melted butter or mayonnaise, most people think artichokes are fattening but they are low in calorie and high in nutrition. I made the following dipping sauce and tried it with my steamed artichoke. I made it again the next night and spooned it over grilled asparagus. It was fantastic and my family loved it!

Another idea for dipping artichokes or any raw vegetable is to add a variety
of herbs and seasonings to a small container or plain Greek yogurt and mixing well! We like it with a robust blend of Mediterranean herbs.

DIPPING SAUCE FOR STEAMED ARTICHOKES
Maintenance Phase

1 Lemon, juiced
2-3 Tsp. Capers
2-3 Tbl. Extra-Virgin Olive Oil

Mix all ingredients in a small bowl or ramekin and serve as a dip with
steamed Artichokes or as a topping for steamed or grilled asparagus.
Use 2 Tbl. of the Olive oil to start with and taste it.
Add a little bit more oil at a time until it tastes good, as lemons can
vary in tartness and juiciness!

Recipe makes enough dip for 2 small or medium artichokes or as a
drizzle over 1 lb. asparagus.

Open any cookbook today and you'll find at least one or two fish marinade recipes. Most of the ones in my books have some amount of sugar or too much added fat, so I mixed up a batch of this marinade using ingredients that were in my fridge while making dinner one night. The fresh fish I bought sat in the marinade for an hour or so before going on the grill. We thought it was delicious.

FISH MARINADE
Maintenance Phase

1 Clove Garlic, crushed
Juice of 1 small or ½ medium/large Lemon
1/2 – 1 Tsp. Dijon Mustard
2 Tbl. Extra-virgin Olive Oil
1 Tbl. Tarragon, fresh chopped and/or Dill or 1 tsp. of each dried
1 Tbl. Capers
Season to taste

Crush garlic into a small bowl.
Add lemon juice, mustard, oil and mix well.
Add salt, herbs and capers, mix again.
Spoon or brush mixture onto fish at least 30 minutes before cooking, and reserve extra mixture to baste the fish with as it cooks.

Recipe makes enough marinade for 3-4 servings of fresh fish, 6-8 oz fillets.

My grandmother lived to the age of 96, as did my grandfather. My dad swears it's because they loved to eat her fresh beet horseradish, prepared the traditional Russian way. Her horseradish was so strong that the container had to be kept covered on the dinner table when it was served or we'd cry from the vapors!

It's still a family favorite, and this condiment is great on everything from roast beef to chilled "gefilte" fish.

GRANDMA'S BEET HORSERADISH
Maintenance Phase

1 Cup Horseradish, finely grated
1 Medium Beet, fresh, finely grated
$\frac{1}{2}$ Tsp. Sea Salt or Kosher Salt
$\frac{1}{2}$ Tsp. Truvia sweetener
3 Tbl. Cider Vinegar

Peel and grate horseradish and keep it covered while grating the peeled beet. Mix them together.
Add salt, Truvia and enough vinegar to make juice, adjusting amount as necessary to keep the mixture moist.
Fill jar or other airtight container and refrigerate.

Recipe makes one 8 oz. jar.

I used to follow a diet that allowed me to eat Steel Cut Oatmeal in the morning. I needed something to mix into it during the second week on my new diet to keep me interested in eating breakfast. A friend mentioned that she mixed in fresh fruit and roasted chopped almonds into hers. I thought that sounded great, and it was! The problem I foresaw was that it was already mid-summer and fresh berries and stone fruits (ones with pits) were going to be out of season soon. What could I do to ensure that I'd have goodies to stir into my oatmeal every morning? I could make fresh fruit preserves without sugar! That was it. My kitchen became a jam factory for nearly 3 weeks! Every free evening I made another variety; strawberry, apricot, blueberry, peach, strawberry-raspberry, cherry, even lemon! Jars and jars of jam were stacked in my cupboard to use all fall and winter long. Making jam is very easy and it's a fun kid-friendly activity.

We used to mix our jam into the oatmeal during the last 2 minutes of cooking time, now we only mix it into plain yogurt. Once you've tried homemade, you won't want to eat store-bought jam again!

HOMEMADE FRUIT JAM
Maintenance Phase

Follow standard jam recipes inside box of No Sugar Needed Fruit
Pectin but use Truvia, slowly stirring in about half the amount of
sugar called for in the recipes. Start tasting the jam after adding
some of the Truvia while it's cooking; add more until desired
sweetness is reached. Process and seal the jars according to the
Pectin box recipe instructions.

Serving ideas:
Add 1-2 Tbl. as a mix-in with plain non-fat Yogurt, and add 1 packet
or less of Truvia for sweeter tasting Yogurt.
Use as a filling for an omelet using 1 whole egg and 2 egg whites.

ITALIAN STYLE BRUSCHETTA
Maintenance Phase

4-6 Roma tomatoes, finely diced
2 Tbl. Basil, fresh chopped
1-2 Cloves Garlic, fresh crushed or finely minced more or less to taste
1-2 Tsp. Red Onion, finely minced if desired
2 Tsp. Balsamic Vinegar
1 Tbl. Extra-Virgin Olive Oil
Season to taste
1/8 Tsp. Red Chili Flakes if desired
1-2 Tsp. Capers if desired

Chop or mince each of the first 4 ingredients and place in a bowl.
Add vinegar, oil, salt, chili flakes and capers to taste.
Mix well.
Taste mixture to adjust amount of seasonings, and to test spiciness of the garlic and chili flakes.

Salad dressing is one of the things I have a love/hate relationship with. I love full-fat dressings but hate the extra pounds they add to my body! This recipe for Red Wine Vinaigrette is based on traditional preparations, but is lower in fat. No worries, it is still delicious and heart-healthy!

RED WINE VINAIGRETTE
Maintenance Phase

3-4 oz. Red Wine Vinegar (or Cider, White wine, Tarragon, Rice or Balsamic)
1 Tsp. Dijon Mustard
2 Tbl. Lemon juice
1 Clove Garlic, crushed
1 Tbl. Basil, fresh chopped or 1 tsp. dried Italian herbs
Season to taste
3-5 oz. Extra-Virgin Olive Oil or more to taste

Crush garlic, add vinegar, Dijon mustard, Lemon juice, herbs and salt, shake or mix well.
Add oil and mix again. $\frac{1}{4}$ tsp. or more Truvia may be added if desired.

Recipe makes enough dressing for 3-4 dinner salads.

SUSAN'S HOMEMADE SEAFOOD COCKTAIL SAUCE
Maintenance Phase

2/3 C **Organic** Ketchup
3 Tsp. Worchester Sauce
5 Tbl. Lemon juice
1/2 Tsp. Chili Powder
1 Tsp. Old Bay seasoning
4 – 6 shakes of Tabasco Sauce to taste
Mix well.

Recipe makes 1 C sauce.
1 serving = 2 Tbl.

Note:
Use Organic Ketchup to avoid High Fructose Corn Syrup.

TOMATILLO SALSA
Maintenance Phase

15-16 Green Tomatillos
1-2 Jalapeno Peppers
2 Tbl. Canola Oil
$\frac{1}{2}$-1 Cup Water

Peel leaves from the Tomatillos, and wash thoroughly and trim the stems of the Jalapeno peppers.
Place all the Tomatillos and the peppers into a 12" skillet and add water.
Cover and bring to a boil.
Once everything is fully cooked, drain all the water.
Place $\frac{1}{2}$ of the Tomatillos in a food processor and add one pepper, diced and seeded.
Add 1 Tbl. Canola oil and process until smooth.
Pour the mixture into a large bowl and then repeat the process.
It is optional to strain the sauce to remove all the Tomatillo seeds for a smooth consistency.

Recipe makes 4 cups of strained Tomatillo Salsa.

Entrees for Lunch or Dinner

The term for grilled steak in Spanish is Carne Asada, however it is truly much more than that. The term also refers to the full-flavored marinade that gives the meat, or chicken called Pollo Asado, its unique and delightful taste. Soak a lean, thinly cut portion of beef or boneless, skinless chicken for several hours, and then fire up the grill and cook until done. Serve in whole portions, or chop up the meat and serve with guacamole and fresh salsa with a side of whole cooked pinto or black beans. Whether you like your food spicy or mildly seasoned, call Carne Asada "dinner" tonight!

CARNE ASADA
Maintenance Phase

1-1/2 lbs. Flap Steak or any thin-cut beef
3 Tbl. Canola Oil
3 Tbl. Olive Oil
¼ Cup Red Wine vinegar
1 Cup Onion, chopped
1 Lemon, juiced
1 Lime, juiced
1 Yellow Chili Pepper, finely minced
1 Jalapeno chili pepper, finely minced
1 Tbl. New Mexico Chili Powder, ground
Season to taste

Mix ingredients and marinate for 3-6 hours.
Grill over medium flame, turning once until cooked medium or medium well done.
Slice the meat into strips and serve with guacamole and fresh tomato salsa.

Recipe makes 4 servings.

Variation:
Use skinless, boneless chicken in place of the meat.

Talk about a flavorful dish! This curried chicken recipe will knock your socks off. It makes a beautiful presentation for dinner parties, even the ones around your kitchen table on a Tuesday night.

I like to serve this entrée with cooked baby carrots and seasoned steamed lentils topped with a dollop of plain yogurt.

CURRIED CHICKEN
Maintenance Phase

4 Chicken Breasts, skinless with ribs
½ Cup Chicken Broth or Stock
2 Large Onions, sliced in rings
2 Cloves Garlic, crushed
4 Tbl. Sugar-free Apricot Jam (tip: see Homemade Jam recipe)
2 Oz. White Vinegar
2 Tsp. Curry Powder
1 Cup Water
Season to taste

Heat the broth to medium temperature in a heavy sauté pan (use a pan that has a lid).
Add chicken and cook, turning, about 10 minutes until browned.
Add onion and garlic and cook until the onion is clear, about 3 minutes.
Remove chicken onto a plate, and drain the excess liquid from the pan.
Return chicken to the pan and sprinkle it with seasonings to taste.
Mix together apricot jam, vinegar and curry powder in a small bowl, stir in water.
Pour mixture over the chicken and bring to a boil. Reduce heat to low and cover, simmer about 20 minutes or until a fork can be inserted with ease and the juices are clear.
Remove lid and continue to cook about 5 minutes more to reduce liquid.

Recipe makes 4 servings.

Additional items:
Add 4 large peeled carrots, cut into chunks.
Garnish cooked chicken with chopped or sliced unsalted roasted almonds, and 1 Tbl. raisins, any color.

Chili Con Carne is one of those one pot wonders that have sustained generation after generation of Americans, through good times and lean ones. Its hearty flavor and filling ingredients have inspired cooking contests throughout the Southwestern United States and can be prepared hot and spicy or mildly seasoned, with or without beans and plenty of rib-sticking meat.

Ground turkey has replaced fattier ground beef in this recipe, and the beans should be home-cooked to ensure freshness without too much sodium or starchiness.

EASY TURKEY CHILI
Maintenance Phase

4 Cups Home-cooked Beans; White, Pinto, Kidney or Black or a combination
1. Can Ready-cut Tomatoes, 28 oz., reserve juice
1 Can Tomato Sauce, 14 oz.
2 Tbl. Chili Powder
1 Medium White Onion, diced
2-1/2 lbs. Ground Turkey
2 Cloves garlic, crushed
Cayenne (Red) Pepper to taste
3 Tbl. Canola Oil
$\frac{1}{4}$ Cup Water or Chicken Broth
Season to taste

Brown chopped onion and garlic in oil in a heavy skillet.
Remove and set aside.
Brown the ground turkey in the same skillet.
Mix in all the other ingredients, including the onions and garlic.
Cook uncovered for 1 hour.
Add juice from ready-cut tomatoes as needed while cooking.
Cook longer if thicker chili is desired.

Recipe makes 10 servings.

Additional ingredient ideas:
Add $\frac{1}{2}$ Tsp. ground cumin and/or oregano.
Add 4 oz. Anaheim chili peppers, roasted and diced.
Add 1 chopped Bell Pepper.
Add 1 Cup fresh corn, shucked off the cob; raw or pre-cooked.
Substitute 1 small (6 oz.) can tomato paste for the tomato sauce; add 1 additional cup water or chicken broth.
Garnish with chopped scallion greens.

The classic French white bean stew called "Cassoulet" is delicious but extremely fattening. This recipe for Lemon-Tarragon Chicken Cassoulet is incredibly delicious and good for you without all the fat, plus its fun to make and to serve when you've got a crowd for dinner.

I've made this recipe in the crock pot (I have an oval shaped one designed to cook a whole chicken) and in a "French" oven which is a fancy name for a covered pot that also is oval shaped. You can cook this dish in any heavy pot with a lid that can be placed in the oven. I like making it when the weather is bad and I plan to be home for a few hours, as there are a number of ingredients that are to be added during each phase of the cooking process.

Serve this dish with a side salad and some fresh fruit for dessert.

Bon Appetite!

LEMON TARRAGON CHICKEN CASSOULET
Maintenance Phase

1 Whole Chicken
4-6 cloves garlic, whole
3 stalks fresh Tarragon, chopped or 3 Tbl. Dried Tarragon
1 onion, chopped
3 Medium Carrots, sliced in thick chunks
2 Cups Beans; home cooked, small white Navy beans or Black-Eyed Peas
2 Cups Green Beans, whole or sliced
2 Cups Mushrooms, whole
3 Lemons, sliced in half
½ Cup White Wine; any dry variety but use one you'd like enough to drink!
1 Cup Chicken Broth
Season to taste

Clean chicken inside and out and season well.
Place chicken in a Dutch or French oven or heavy pot with lid.
Slice lemons in half and stuff the cavity of the chicken with as many as will
fit inside.
Bake at 350 degrees for 20 minutes uncovered.
Add the remaining lemons, wine, broth Tarragon, garlic, onions and carrots to the pot.
Bake covered for 20 minutes.
Add beans and mushrooms; continue cooking for another 10 minutes.
Add green beans and cook for another 10 minutes.
Remove the chicken from the pot and cut into pieces, removing skin; place the chicken in a large serving bowl.
Remove all the vegetables and beans from the pot with a slotted spoon and surround the chicken with them. Drain all the pan juices into a gravy-fat separator or into a 4-cup measuring cup.
Remove as much of the fat as possible, and pour the remaining juices over the chicken and vegetables.

Recipe makes 4 - 6 servings

I had some thick boneless pork chops in the freezer and needed a simple and quick way to prepare them one night for dinner. I also had some Roma tomatoes and fresh basil in the vegetable bin and had thought about making a batch of Bruschetta earlier that day. Wait a minute. What if I made the Bruschetta to use as a condiment for the meat; then cooked the chops on the stove using some of the same ingredients? Oooh, this was going to be a winner. And it was!

PORK CHOPS ITALIAN STYLE
Maintenance Phase

2 Six-ounce Pork Chops, boneless and trimmed
1-2 Tbl. Canola Oil
½ Cups Balsamic Vinegar
1-2 Cloves Garlic, crushed
Season to taste
½ Cup Bruschetta, prepared in advance

Season pork chops and set aside.
Coat the bottom of a sauté pan with Canola oil.
Heat over medium flame, and add garlic; cooking until it becomes translucent. Add vinegar and bring to a boil.
Turn down the heat and add pork chops.
Cook the chops long enough to be done on one side.
Turn them and continue cooking until the meat is cooked but still juicy.
Remove from pan and slice into strips. Fan the meat on the plate and top with fresh Bruschetta (see the recipe on page 55).

Recipe makes 2 servings.

ROSEMARY CHICKEN
Maintenance Phase

3 Chicken breasts, whole boneless and skinless or 6 half-breasts

3-4 Cloves Garlic, crushed or finely chopped

1 Stalk Rosemary, fresh, or 1 Tbl. Rosemary, dried

$\frac{1}{4}$ Cup Dry White Wine, use one you would like well enough to drink

$\frac{1}{4}$ Cup Chicken Broth

Season to taste

Preheat broiler.

Season the Chicken.

Place chicken seasoned with garlic, rosemary; wine and broth in a Dutch oven or large, deep skillet.

Cook covered over medium heat about 30 minutes or until tender, turning once.

Recipe makes 6 servings.

SEAFOOD STEW
Maintenance Phase

4 C Seafood Stock
½-3/4 lb. Crab (King, Dungeness or Snow, in shell)
½ lb. Mussels
½ lb. Clams
½ lb. Shrimp, peeled and deveined
1 Filet of fresh fish, diced
1 Onion, diced
2-4 Cloves Garlic, fresh, chopped to taste
2 Stalks Celery, diced
2 T Canola or Extra-virgin Olive Oil
Season to taste

Heat oil in stock pot and add garlic, onion and celery.
Cook until soft.
Add stock and seasonings, bring to a boil.
Reduce heat to low, and add crab for about 5 minutes.
Add mussels and clams; cover and cook for another 3 minutes.
Add shrimp and continue cooking until fish is cooked and clams and mussels open, about 2-3 more minutes.
Remove crab and slice open the legs vertically in half to make it easy to remove the meat, return crab to the pot. This dish can be served from the pot, or can be transferred to a large deep bowl.

Recipe makes 3-4 six-ounce portions depending on the yield of the shellfish, size of the shrimp and weight of the fish fillet.

Soups

The following recipe is for traditional chicken soup, minus the bay leaf you sometimes see in recipes simply because my grandmothers never used it and my family isn't crazy for the flavor it imparts to the soup. The reason it is in the Maintenance recipe section is because it calls for carrots which are not on the HCG Phase diet list of vegetables.

Whether you enjoy the traditional version, or add extra vegetables and Tomatillo sauce to your pot of chicken soup, it will warm your body, comfort whatever ails you and satisfy your rumbling tummy!

CHICKEN SOUP
Maintenance Phase

1 Whole Chicken, Kosher preferred, washed thoroughly
3 Stalks Celery, trimmed
1 Yellow Onion, peeled and quartered
3 Whole Carrots, peeled and trimmed
1 Bunch Parsley, kept together with a rubber band or string
Season to taste

Place washed chicken in an 8 qt. pot and fill with water until the chicken is almost covered.
Bring to a boil for 20-30 minutes.
Skim the scum that forms at the top of the pot.
Reduce the heat to medium and continue boiling uncovered for another 15 minutes.
Add 3 whole stalks celery, 3 large carrots, one quartered yellow onion and a whole bunch of parsley.
Cover and reduce heat to low, simmering for 40 minutes.
Remove chicken, and continue to simmer uncovered on medium heat for another 15 minutes.
Remove all the vegetables and skim well to remove fat and residue from the broth.
Dice carrots and remove bones and skin from chicken.
Return the chicken and carrots to the soup before serving.

Note:
If you don't need to serve this soup immediately, refrigerate it until the fat hardens, then remove it!

CHICKEN TOMATILLO VEGETABLE SOUP
Maintenance Phase

1 Whole Chicken, Kosher preferred, washed thoroughly
3 Stalks Celery, trimmed
1 Yellow Onion, peeled and quartered
3 Carrots, peeled and trimmed
2 Whole Zucchini, cut into thick chunks
1 Bunch Cilantro, kept together with a rubber band or string
1 lb. Mushrooms, any variety, trimmed
4 Cups Tomatillo Salsa
Season to taste

Place washed chicken in an 8 qt. pot and fill with water until the chicken is almost covered.
Bring to a boil for 20-30 minutes.
Skim the scum that forms at the top of the pot.
Reduce the heat to medium and continue boiling uncovered for another 15 minutes.
Add whole stalks celery, carrots, zucchini chunks, one quartered yellow onion, mushrooms and a bunch of cilantro.
Cover and reduce heat to low, simmering for 40 minutes.
Remove chicken, add seasonings and Tomatillo Salsa and continue to simmer uncovered on medium heat for another 15 minutes.
When the chicken is cool, remove the bones and skin.
Return the chicken to the soup.
Cook for another 5 minutes uncovered.
Skim all the fat before serving.

Note:
If you don't need to serve this soup immediately, refrigerate it overnight until the fat hardens, then remove it!

My cousin and I both worked downtown in San Diego for many years. One of the first restaurants she took me to in 1983 was "Athen's Market", owned by the marvelous Mary Pappas. Mary made her father's recipe for lentil soup one of her signature dishes, and prepares it every day. Mary never told me what was in the recipe that gave it such a special flavor, but I had my theories.

I get together with my neighbors every few months, and it was my turn to host the crowd so I decided to make soup and a variety of salads for dinner. I experimented until I thought I'd captured the essence of it, and decided to give the lentil soup a try in the crock pot. It was a hit with my friends, and none of it was left over. In fact, one neighbor sent an email thanking me for the evening, and requested the recipe!

GREEK STYLE LENTIL SOUP
Maintenance Phase

1 16 oz. package lentils (3 cups)
4 Cups water
7 Cloves Garlic, finely diced or minced
1 Can 29 oz. and 1 can 14 oz. Tomato Sauce OR 12 processed fresh
Roma Tomatoes plus 1 small can Tomato Paste mixed with 8 oz. Water
3 Tbl. Oregano, dried
1/4 C White Vinegar
Salt to taste (I add 4-6 large pinches of Kosher or ground sea salt
when   using fresh tomatoes. If your canned sauce contains sodium,
you may want   to use less salt)

Rinse lentils and place in 5 qt. pot, pour water over the lentils.
Cover, bring to a boil and then reduce to simmer.
Add tomato sauce, garlic, oregano and vinegar and continue to simmer
covered for 45 minutes stirring occasionally.
Add salt, more vinegar, water and spices/seasonings as desired and
continue cooking for 20-30 minutes.

One serving of this soup is 2/3 cup.

MINESTRONE SOUP
Maintenance Phase

1 Onion, large, chopped
3 Stalks of celery, sliced into $\frac{1}{2}$" thick pieces on the diagonal or diced
1 Clove of garlic, minced
4 Cups home-cooked kidney beans with 2 cups bean broth
2 Cups home-cooked Garbanzo beans
3-4 Carrots, sliced into $\frac{1}{2}$" thick pieces on the diagonal or diced
5 Zucchini, sliced into $\frac{1}{2}$" thick pieces on the diagonal or diced
6 Cups water or Chicken Broth
(3 Tsp. of "Better Than Bullion" Chicken flavor if using water)
3 Cups Marinara sauce
1 Cup Tomato Sauce
Herbs: Oregano, Basil, Marjoram, 1 Tsp. ground Cumin, freshly ground
Black Pepper, Cayenne Pepper and Salt to taste
1 large splash of Red Wine if desired

Use 1 Cup of Chicken broth to poach the onions and celery. When the onion is soft, add garlic but don't let it brown.
Add Garbanzo beans, all the bean broth and half of the Kidney beans to the cooked vegetable mixture.
Puree the remaining Kidney beans in a food processor and add to the pot.
Add carrots, zucchini, water or prepared "Better Than Bullion" or soup stock, marinara and tomato sauce, and all the herbs; fresh or dried.
Simmer all for 3 hours or longer if a thicker soup is desired.
Taste and correct the seasonings if necessary.

Garnish:
Freshly grated Parmesan cheese
Freshly chopped parsley

Recipe makes a large pot of soup; servings can range from 10 to 12 oz.

Optional Ingredients:
Chicken Basil Sausage and/or Ground Turkey
Cabbage or Spinach

Slice one package of basil sausage, sauté until browned. Add to the pot when the beans and sauce are added.

Cook 12-16 oz. of ground Turkey in a skillet and season well with salt, pepper and garlic powder until browned. Small turkey meatballs can also be formed and browned. Add meat to the pot when the beans and sauce are added. The addition of ground Turkey will also help to thicken the soup.

Chop fresh cabbage or spinach and add to the pot during the last 15 minutes of cooking.

Vegetables and Beans

There is a great restaurant in Poway, CA called "Dominic's". Dominic is there, in the kitchen and greeting guests most evenings. His place is family oriented, meaning that when you're there, you're family. Moments after being seated, his guests are treated to a few snacks, including his famous "dough knots", bits of twisted pizza dough baked with olive oil and garlic and a plate of thinly sliced carrots marinated in an olive oil and fresh oregano mixture with a bit of garlic and a touch of balsamic vinegar.

Oh, those carrots are divine. I didn't ask him for the recipe, but nonetheless figured out the basics and reproduced it using a bit less oil but hope you'll find them tasty and enjoyable just the same!

ITALIAN STYLE MARINATED CARROTS
Maintenance Phase

1 lb. Carrots, peeled and thinly sliced
1/8 Cup Balsamic Vinegar
1/8 Cup Red Wine Vinegar
2 Tbl. Extra-Virgin Olive Oil
1 Tbl. Oregano, fresh chopped or $\frac{1}{2}$ Tsp. dried Oregano
1 Tbl. Basil, fresh chopped
2 Garlic, large cloves, crushed or minced

Thinly slice fresh carrots, place them in a non-aluminum mixing bowl.
Mix remaining ingredients and pour over the carrots and let stand for
30 minutes.
Allow them to marinate in the refrigerator for 8 hours or overnight.
Serve either cold or room temperature.

Recipe makes 4-5 servings.

Alternate preparation:
Boil sliced carrots for 3 minutes to soften carrots before marinating.

Variation:
Use Raspberry vinegar in place of Balsamic and Red Wine vinegars.

Mexican restaurants of all sizes, shapes and variety abound throughout Southern California, and many of them feature a salsa bar where patrons can help themselves to a variety of sauces from very mild to extremely hot and spicy. Often there will be a bin of carrots with sliced onions and jalapeno peppers in a vinegar based marinade that is really good!

Once again, I just experimented until the taste was familiar.

Buen Provecho!

MEXICAN STYLE MARINATED CARROTS
Maintenance Phase

1 lb. Carrots, peeled and thinly sliced
1/2 Cup White vinegar
2 Tbl. Extra-virgin Olive Oil
1 Tbl. Oregano, fresh chopped or 1 Tsp. dried oregano or
1 Whole White Onion, finely sliced
3 Tbl. to 1/3 Cup Jalapeno Peppers, canned, sliced
1 Tbl. Truvia sweetener if desired
Season to taste

Thinly slice fresh carrots, boil in water for 3 minutes, strain.
Place them in a non-aluminum mixing bowl.
Mix remaining ingredients and pour over the carrots and let stand for 30 minutes.
Taste the mixture and adjust seasonings as desired.
Allow them to marinate in the refrigerator for 8 hours or overnight.
Serve either cold or room temperature.

Recipe makes 4-5 servings.

A familiar rhyme was often uttered at the mere mention of beans when I was a child. Undeterred by the warning of their effect, I couldn't imagine eating a Mexican meal without the comforting presence of refried beans on my plate! They were very fattening and unhealthy to say the least. Today many restaurants use vegetable oil to make their refried beans which is certainly healthier, though the taste and consistency isn't the same.

I have come to love best the beans that are prepared with the fewest ingredients. Whole pinto beans cooked with fresh water, a few whole cloves of garlic, even a couple of whole Jalapeno peppers and enough salt to flavor the beans near the end of the cooking process is all it takes! Eat them whole with plenty of the natural juice-gravy, or process them partially with or without the cooked garlic and Jalapenos using just the liquid from the beans. Some people love cracked pepper added to them. Either way you'll get plenty of nutrients, fiber and flavor!

THREE BEAN SALAD
Maintenance Phase

1 Cup Dried Black-Eyed Peas
1 Cup Dried Garbanzo Beans
1 Cup Kidney Beans
1 Bell Pepper, any color or combination
½ Cup Carrots, diced or chopped if desired
½ Cup Tomatoes or Pimentos, diced if desired
1 Cup Red Wine Vinaigrette (see recipe on page 56)
Season to taste
Truvia sweetener to taste if desired

Soak the beans in a large pot with water covering the beans plus at least 1-2" of water above the beans overnight or for 8 hours.
Drain all the water and replace with fresh water.
Bring the pot of beans to a boil and cook until all are firm but fully done.
Chop all the vegetables and tomatoes.
Drain the beans and rinse well.
Place all the ingredients into a large bowl and mix well.
Refrigerate until chilled before serving.

Recipe makes about 5 cups; or 10 servings.

Acknowledgements

Many years ago, my Aunt Bonnie told me that she preferred to eat to live, not live to eat. That idea has stuck with me, and I've thought a lot about the difference between her attitude toward food and mine. Heck, I sit in restaurants with family and friends waiting for lunch to be served, and talk about what I'm going to prepare for dinner that night! My relationship with food has always been an issue, as it's a very important one to me!

My friend of over 4 decades, Laura Katleman, has written a wonderful new book called "Skinny Thinking" about her battle with weight and how she changed her relationship with food to become a healthy eater, leaving behind old notions and habits that lead to being overweight. Her book teaches anyone how to move through the stages of becoming a wise eater, with concepts and directions that are helping me to reconsider my own thoughts, feelings and eating habits, and I trust that her process works. Thank you, Laura, for your ideas, experience, and support with this project.

Special thanks to Dr. and Mrs. Mayer Eisenstein for sharing the success of their new "Homefirst HCG Metabolic Syndrome Weight Loss Program" featuring Low Glycemic Index foods, sublingual doses of his proprietary liquid HCG and a variety of dietary supplements and a very low calorie diet and maintenance program with us, and for all your support during these past months while the belly fat that caused my liver disease just melted away, leaving my liver clear of fatty deposits! Visit his website at **www.homefirst.com** for more information or a referral to a participating physician in your area.

Thank you to my friend Kathleen Day, who designed the recipe format and typed several of these recipes into her laptop computer while I prepared them.

To Mark and Dina who inspire me daily in all my endeavors; and to Mom for all your good advice; I lovingly thank you!

15918814R00048

Made in the USA
Lexington, KY
24 June 2012